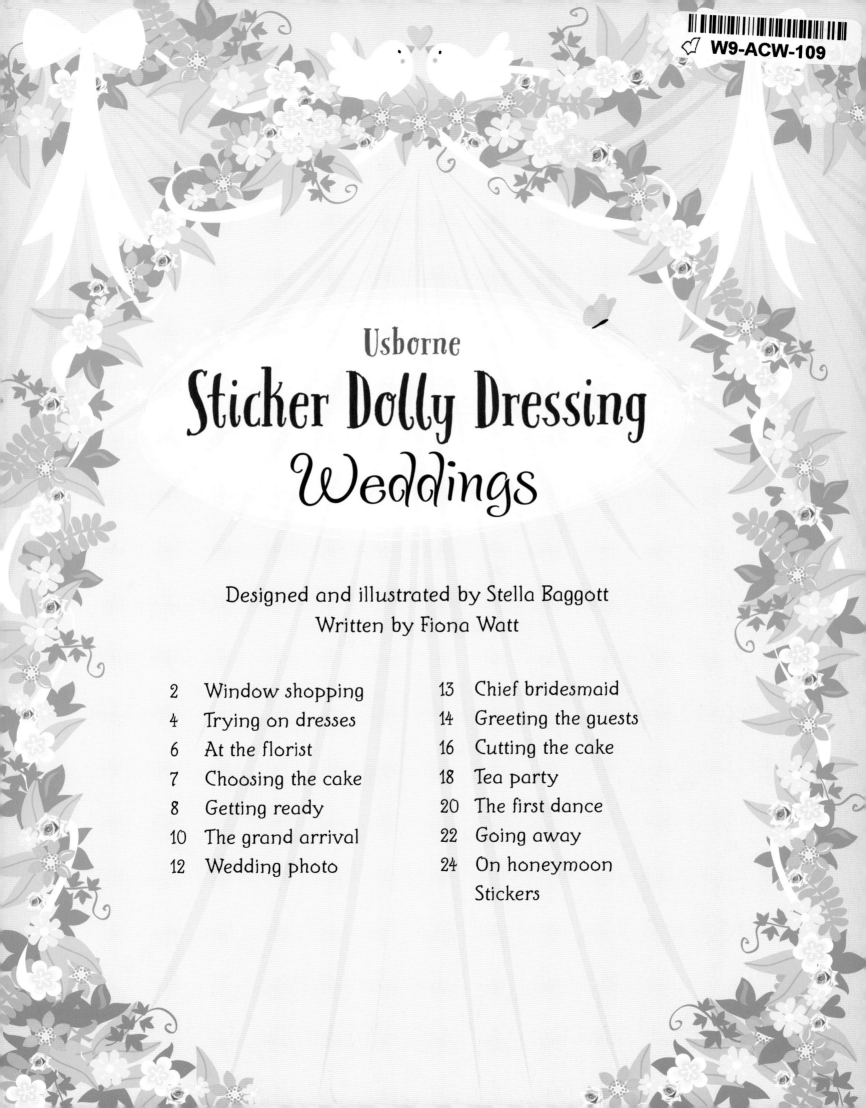

Usborne
Sticker Dolly Dressing
Weddings

Designed and illustrated by Stella Baggott
Written by Fiona Watt

Window shopping

Abi, Lily and Bea have been asked to be bridesmaids for their best friend, Polly. She has asked them to look at dresses in bridal shops to see if they can find a style that will suit them all.

Trying on dresses

Tess is having a final fitting for her wedding dress. She has tried it on before, but it was too long so now the hem has been taken up. Kirstie and Ella are excited to be trying on their bridesmaids' outfits, too.

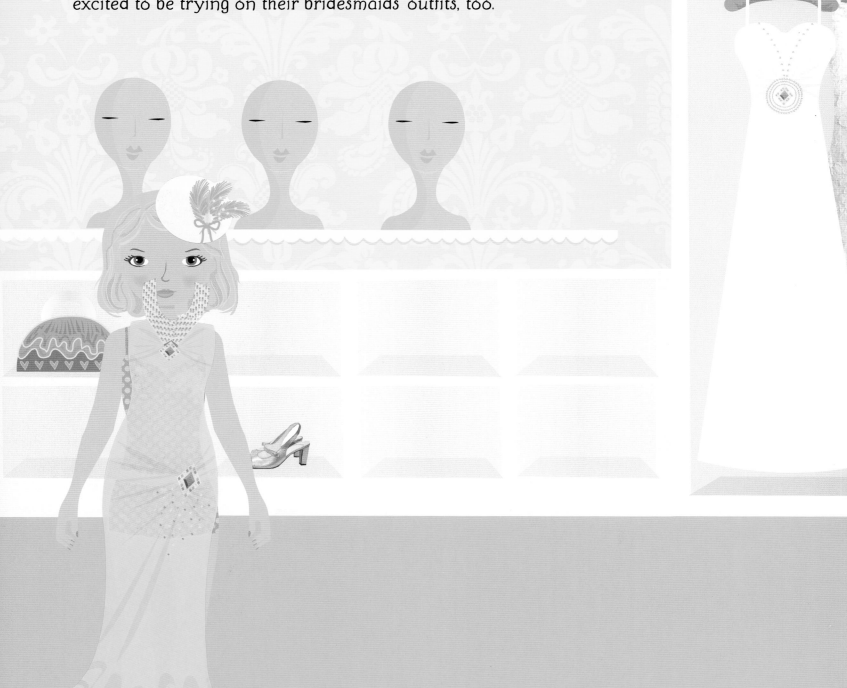

At the florist

Maria has had an appointment with the florist who is helping her to choose the bouquet that she will carry on her wedding day. She has decided upon delicate white and yellow roses, surrounded by wispy green leaves.

Choosing the cake

Gabriella has just become engaged. Her wedding is next year, but she is already looking for the type of cake she would like. She has seen a beautiful one with three layers, decorated with fresh flowers.

Getting ready

Victoria and her bridesmaids, Kaitlin and Mia, have had their hair styled and have done their own make up. The girls help Victoria put on her wedding dress first, then get themselves ready.

The grand arrival

Izzy has always dreamed of going to her wedding in a fairytale carriage pulled by horses ... and now her wish has come true. Her mother and her bridesmaid, Chloe, have made sure that her elegant dress didn't get crushed while she was sitting in the carriage.

Wedding photo

The ceremony is over. Lizzie has been asked by the wedding photographer to pose in the grounds of the countryhouse where she has just been married.

Chief bridesmaid

Maddie's a bridesmaid at her best friend's wedding.
She's taking a walk in the garden after the ceremony,
while the bride and groom are having their photo
taken with their little flower girls.

Greeting the guests

David and Emily have arrived at their reception in a grand hotel. They're now waiting to thank all the guests for coming to their wedding, before sitting down for the speeches, followed by a sumptuous meal.

Cutting the cake

Tanya and Robbie's wedding meal is over and the speeches have been given. It's now time for them to cut their cake. Traditionally, this is the first task that a newly married couple perform together as husband and wife.

Tea party

Lauren and Jack have had a quiet wedding with only a few of their close relatives at the ceremony. For their reception, they've arranged a tea party, rather than having a grand, sit-down meal. Lauren's friends, Maya and Emma, have just arrived with presents for the happy couple.

The first dance

The band start playing as Joshua and Sam take to the floor for that special moment - their first dance together as husband and wife. They have chosen music that is very special to them and will treasure the memory of this dance forever.

Going away

The guests have gathered outside the reception. Sara loves wearing her wedding dress so much she hasn't changed for the send off. Just before they leave, Sara will throw her bouquet over her shoulder for one of her girlfriends to catch.

On honeymoon

The excitement of the wedding is over, and Isaac and Katy are relaxing on a tropical island honeymoon. As well as lounging on the beach, they have driven around the island and have been diving on a coral reef. Today they are going for a picnic on a yacht.

Additional design and illustration by Vici Leyhane and Molly Sage.

This edition first published in 2020 by Usborne Publishing Ltd, 83-85 Saffron Hill, London, EC1N 8RT, England. www.usborne.com